# THE ORACLE BOOK

## Answers to Life's Questions

GEORGIA ROUTSIS SAVAS

*Illustrations by Melanie Marder Parks*

**BANTAM BOOKS**

LONDON • NEW YORK • TORONTO • SYDNEY • AUCKLAND

*ALSO BY*

# GEORGIA ROUTSIS SAVAS

*Total Astrology:*
*What the Stars Say About Life and Love*

## THE ORACLE BOOK
## A BANTAM BOOK : 0 553 81488 5

First publication in Great Britain

Originally published in the US by Simon & Schuster, Inc.

PRINTING HISTORY
Bantam edition published 2002

1 3 5 7 9 10 8 6 4 2

Bantam Books are published by Transworld Publishers,
61–63 Uxbridge Road, London W5 5SA,
a division of The Random House Group Ltd,
in Australia by Random House Australia (Pty) Ltd,
20 Alfred Street, Milsons Point, Sydney, NSW 2061, Australia,
in New Zealand by Random House New Zealand Ltd,
18 Poland Road, Glenfield, Auckland 10, New Zealand
and in South Africa by Random House (Pty) Ltd,
Endulini, 5a Jubilee Road, Parktown 2193, South Africa.

Printed and bound in Great Britain by
Mackays of Chatham plc, Chatham, Kent.

www.**books**at**trans**world.co.uk

# ACKNOWLEDGMENTS

THIS BOOK OWES ITS EXISTENCE TO THE FOLLOWING FOLKS: To my editor, Amanda Murray, for her gracious guidance (and for instinctively pitching this project to me, the Queen of Divining). To Simon & Schuster, for putting this book together and for coming up with an extraordinary visual package. To Ruth Sullivan, the wise woman of publishing, for her help and expertise. To JR Watson, for his semi-rational assistance. To my grandmother, Anna Skunakis, who introduced me to soothsaying. To my parents, Gus and Stella Routsis, for supplying my genetic blueprint (for better or for worse). To Savannah, for her canine intuition. And to my husband, Damon, for his ironclad support, never-ending patience . . . and just about everything else.

# INTRODUCTION

"What should I do?" is a question that just about every living, breathing human being has asked at some point in his or her life. Some folks ask family and friends for advice, others seek guidance from a therapist, still others call upon a psychic or astrologer to illuminate the situation. No matter the method used in this world of I-wanted-it-yesterday, people want their answers delivered quickly. ∞ THERE ARE HUNDREDS, if not thousands, of divination techniques available that give pretty near instant answers. They range from the familiar, like Crystallomancy (using a crystal ball), to the more obscure, like Capnomancy (the study of smoke rising from a fire). By using *The Oracle Book* you'll be practicing a form of Bibliomancy—the answering of a question by means of randomly choosing a word or passage from a book. ∞ THOUGH THE BIBLE was historically the book of choice for Bibliomancy, people have also used ancient Greek epics, poetry or Shakespearean works. Many believe Bibliomancy is the Western world's answer to the *I Ching: The Book of Questions*, a divination system developed by the Chinese over four thousand years ago. When people consult the *I Ching*, they throw yarrow stalks or coins and interpret the way in which they fall as the answer to their question. ∞ NOWADAYS, MOST PEOPLE don't have yarrow stalks handy, or much patience to decipher cryptic messages. That's where *The Oracle Book* comes in. This handy do-it-yourself divination tool takes its name from the oracles of ancient Greece—these were humans who acted as divine intermediaries, delivering messages from the gods to their earthbound peers. But the term "oracle" can also refer to the message itself, a magical glimpse into the future, and that's how it's used here. *The Oracle Book* brings together a wealth of predictions drawn from a variety of ancient and modern divination techniques. Within these pages are predictions drawn from astrology, tarot cards, tea leaves, playing cards, dice, the crystal ball, palmistry and psychic wisdom. ∞ IN ORDER TO get started, first you're going to have to check your logic at the door and rely on your intuition. The truth is that Bibliomancy and other forms of divination aren't really about predicting the future. They are tools that can help guide you to the answer that already lies deep inside yourself. The answer you pick is determined by the exact moment you, and only you, decide to stop flipping through *The Oracle Book*. Somehow, the page with the "right" answer just beckons you to stop. ∞ THERE ARE SOME lucky people who already possess finely tuned intuitive skills. They're the ones who always seem to be in the right place at the right time. But if you're one of those highly evolved souls with a, hmm, "deeply buried intuition," don't despair. Chances are your inner guide is safe and sound. Have you ever turned on the radio to find that the song you've been humming all day happens to be on? Or run into an old acquaintance that you've been thinking about just minutes before? If so, you've got what it takes to get your intuition (back) in shape. All it needs is regular exercise, which is what you'll get by using this book.

# HOW TO USE THE
# ORACLE BOOK

Unlike other forms of divination, with *The Oracle Book* there's no in-depth studying required. No special incantation to memorize, no swami to venerate and no fancy fortune-telling outfit involved—all you need is a few minutes and an open mind. ∽TO BEGIN, HOLD the book in both hands and take a few deep, cleansing breaths. Then concentrate on a yes-or-no question. When your question is clear in your mind, repeat it once (silently or aloud). Then run your thumb (your left if you're left-handed, right if you're right-handed) over the edge of the pages and when you sense your thumb is in the right place, open the book. The answer to your question will be revealed. ∽ SOMETIMES AN ANSWER will make immediate sense and will apply directly to you and your situation. Other times, the advice will seem vague. Pay attention to how you're feeling when you're submitting your query. An imprecise question (or unsure mind) invariably yields an unclear answer. Excuse the cliché, but in divining, practice does make perfect. The more you use this tool, the sharper your intuition gets. And therein lies the secret to finding the ever-elusive "right" answer. ∽

# THE
# ORACLE
## BOOK

# ASTROLOGY

THE MOON,
illuminary of
intuition,
counsels you
to rely on your
first impression.

# TAROT

You've drawn the
KING OF
PENTACLES:
consult a
knowledgeable
authority.

# PSYCHIC

Listen to the
PSYCHİC:
the time is right.

# PALMISTRY

# THE PALM
# READER

sees a cross in the palm,

which indicates

a challenge.

Rise to it.

# TEA LEAVES

# AT THE BOTTOM OF YOUR CUP

is the shape
of a dolphin:
have fun with it.

# CRYSTAL BALL

# THE
# CRYSTAL
# BALL

shows a

setting sun:

time is

running out.

# DICE

# THE DİCE
have come up

triple sixes:

smile,

there is every

indication

of happiness.

ASTROLOGY

# MERCURY,

the planet of intellect,

advises you to

take the

next logical step.

DİCE

# A ROLL OF
# NUMBER
# SEVENTEEN

means

success depends

on perseverance.

# PLAYING CARD

You've drawn
THE FİVE ⊙F
SPADES:
it will be tough.

# TAROT

You've drawn
THE QUEEN OF
PENTACLES:
your prayers will be
answered.

# PSYCHIC

# THE PSYCHIC'S RESPONSE:

only if it will make

you happy.

# PALMISTRY

# THE PALM READER

sees a trident shape
in the palm:
use a more
creative approach.

# TEA LEAVES

# AT THE BOTTOM
## OF YOUR CUP

is the shape of a cat:

don't obsess about it

and it will

come to you.

# CRYSTAL BALL

# THE
# CRYSTAL
# BALL

reveals a bag of coins:
what you wish for
may cost you.

# DICE

# YOU'VE ROLLED NUMBER SIXTEEN:

as long as no hazard is involved.

# ASTROLOGY

VENUS,
the planet of love,
urges you
to follow
your heart.

# PLAYING CARD

You've selected
THE FOUR OF
SPADES:
you already
know the answer.

# TAROT

You've drawn
THE PRINCE OF
PENTACLES:
tell it like it is.

PSYCHIC

# THE PSYCHIC

counsels you
to act prudently.

# PALMISTRY

# THE PALM READER

sees a full mount

of Neptune:

you alone

cannot control

the outcome.

# TAROT

You've drawn the
PRINCESS OF
PENTACLES:
you've already learned
your lesson.

# TEA LEAVES

# THE TEA
# LEAVES

have formed a rose:

the line between

pain and pleasure

is obscured.

# DICE

# THE DÍCE

have come up

triple fives:

only if you

change your

priorities.

# PLAYING CARD

You've selected
THE QUEEN OF
DIAMONDS:
be careful what
you wish for.

# PALMISTRY

THE PALM
READER
sees a deep line
of Apollo:
a dazzling result
is forecast.

# TEA LEAVES

THE TEA
LEAVES
have formed
the shape of a broom:
this is not the time
to be secretive.

CRYSTAL BALL

According to the
CRYSTAL
BALL,
it will bring
you good luck.

DİCE

# YOU'VE ROLLED A FIVE:

providence supports
you as long as you
take care of
yourself.

# ASTROLOGY

NEPTUNE,
the planet of illusion,
warns that you will
be deceived if
you follow through.

# DICE

# YOU'VE ROLLED
# A FOUR:

someone will try to

prevent it

from happening.

# CRYSTAL BALL

The image in
THE
CRYSTAL
BALL
warns you
to proceed
with caution.

# PLAYING CARD

You've

selected

THE TEN OF

DIAMONDS:

be on your

guard.

# PALMISTRY

# THE PALM READER

sees a

frayed heart line,

which means

you need to

focus your

attentions.

TAROT

You've drawn
THE PRİNCE
⊙F WAΠDS:
the winds of change
are blowing
your way.

# PALMISTRY

# THE PALM READER

sees a break

in the life line:

expect an

unexpected

outcome.

PSYCHIC

# THE PSYCHIC
foresees
unexpected travel
related to
your question.

# PLAYING CARD

You've drawn

THE NINE OF

DIAMONDS:

appreciate things

as they are.

# CRYSTAL BALL

The image in
## THE
## CRYSTAL
## BALL
is bright—
move forward
with your plans.

# ✝EA LEAVES

# THE TEA-LEAF
# READER

sees the shape
of an ant:
allow someone
to assist, and you will
achieve victory.

# DİCE

# YOU'VE ROLLED A THREE:

you will succeed
according to
your wish.

# ASTROLOGY

PLUTⵙ,
the planet of
transformation,
commands you
to forget about it.

DICE

# THE DİCE

indicate your
gain will be
significant.

# PLAYING CARD

You've selected
THE EIGHT OF
DIAMONDS:
be more loving and you
will be rewarded.

# CRYSTAL BALL

The image in
THE
CRYSTAL
BALL
is murky—ask
again later.

# PALMISTRY

According to
THE PALM
READER,
the fate line shows
that no one can
prevent it from
happening.

PSYCHIC

# THE
# PSYCHIC
## suggests you
## think it
## through.

# TAROT

You've drawn

THE PRINCESS
OF WANDS:

are you

able to resist?

PSYCHIC

# THE PSYCHIC

says you

must keep

all your

senses alert.

# PLAYING CARD

Your card is

THE SEVEN OF

DIAMONDS:

my, you're feeling

ambitious.

# TEA LEAVES

AT THE BOTTOM
OF YOUR CUP

is the shape of

an umbrella:

you have more

options

than you know.

# CRYSTAL BALL

According to
THE CRYSTAL
BALL,
it's never an
impossibility.

# DICE

# THE DİCE

caution you

to put aside

selfish thoughts

and ask again.

# ASTROLOGY

# THE STARS
# SAY YES—
if you will

respect yourself

in the morning.

DİCE

# YOU'VE ROLLED SNAKE EYES:

it's time to settle your debts.

# CRYSTAL BALL

# THE
# CRYSTAL
# BALL
shows an

open road

ahead.

# ASTROLOGY

A SOLAR
ECLIPSE
hints of
an unexpected
ending.

# TEA LEAVES

# THE TEA
# LEAVES

have taken an

oval shape:

success begins

with positive

thoughts.

# PALMISTRY

According to
THE PALM
READER,
the Apollo
(ring) finger
indicates you
must gamble
to make it happen.

# ASTROLOGY

# THE
# HEAVENLY
# PLANETS

warn that the

risks are great,

but success

will be yours.

# ASTROLOGY

ARIES,

the sign of the Ram,

propels you toward

a positive

outcome.

ASTROLOGY

# THE
# PLANETARY
# FORCES
predict that

good fortune

is in store.

# TAROT

# THE
# FOOL CARD
reminds you that
anything is
possible.

# TAROT

# THE
# JUSTICE
# CARD
is reversed:

forget about it.

# PLAYING CARD

You've selected

THE ACE OF

HEARTS:

a person with

the initial "A"

will make it happen.

# PSYCHIC

# THE PSYCHIC

advises you to

consult a

faraway relative

for advice.

# †EA LEAVES

# THE
# TEA LEAVES
have formed
the shape of a tree:
it will come
to fruition.

# DICE

YOU'VE
ROLLED
A SEVEN,
which forecasts
frustrating delays.

# ASTROLOGY

LIBRA,
the sign of the
Scales,
counsels you
to consider
another's
feelings.

CRYSTAL BALL

# THE
# CRYSTAL
# BALL
promises the

outcome

you desire.

# ASTROLOGY

VIRGO,

the sign of the Virgin,

suggests you

pace yourself—

you'll get there.

# PLAYING CARD

You've drawn
THE JACK OF
HEARTS:
don't plan ahead—
if it's meant to be,
it will just
happen.

TAROT

# THE
# CHARIOT
# CARD

indicates victory

over adversity.

TAROT

# THE
# LOVERS
# CARD

implies that you
cannot avoid it.

# PALMISTRY

# THE PALM
# READER

sees a fork
in the life line:
you'll be happy
either way.

# PLAYING CARD

You've drawn
THE TEN OF
HEARTS:
be patient
and listen.

# TEA LEAVES

# YOUR
# TEA
# LEAVES

show an anchor:
try a change
of scenery.

# TAROT

# THE
# EMPEROR
# CARD

indicates you will

overcome

several obstacles.

TAROT

# THE EMPRESS
## CARD

indicates the answer

will come to you

when you

least expect it.

# DICE

The dice yield
THE
NUMBER
FİVE:
you'll get what
you want
from an unknown
source.

# ASTROLOGY

LEO☉,
THE SIGN
OF THE
LION,
urges you
to enjoy
the limelight
while it lasts.

# TAROT

You've drawn

THE
HIGH
PRIESTESS
CARD:

only you can

answer this

question.

PLAYING CARD

You've drawn
THE SIX OF
HEARTS:
go for it,
but be kind to others
along the way.

# PLAYING CARD

You've selected

THE FOUR

OF HEARTS:

don't be silly.

# ASTROLOGY

CANCER,
THE SIGN OF
THE CRAB,
warns you
to keep your
intentions
to yourself.

# DICE

You've rolled
NUMBER
FOUR,
which indicates
you might be unhappy
with the outcome.

# ASTROLOGY

GEMINI,
THE SIGN OF
THE TWINS,
assures you
can talk
your way into it.

# PLAYING CARD

You've selected
THE THREE
OF HEARTS:
it will change
your image.

# TAROT

# THE
# MAGICIAN
# CARD

warns that
you're taking
an unexpected
risk.

# ASTROLOGY

TAURUS,
THE SIGN OF
THE BULL,
urges you to
act courageously
in the
face of adversity.

# DICE

# YOU'VE ROLLED A NINE:

yes, and you'll

be happier

for it.

TAROT

You've drawn
THE
PRINCESS OF
CUPS CARD:
wait for a secret
to be told.

PLAYING CARD

You've selected
THE KING
OF CLUBS:
it's happening
already.

# CRYSTAL BALL

# THE
# CRYSTAL
# BALL
never lies:

it's definite.

DICE

You've rolled

NUMBER

FIFTEEN:

ask an

acquaintance—

and do

the opposite.

# ASTROLOGY

# THE SUN

urges you

to enjoy

the attention.

# DICE

You've
rolled a
THREE:
most
definitely.

# TEA LEAVES

# THE
# TEA LEAVES

are in the shape

of a shell:

whatever you

desire

shall be yours.

# PALMISTRY

# THE PALM READER

sees an

entrepreneurial

line:

alone

you must

make it happen.

# ASTROLOGY

# PLUTO

urges you to
embrace the
consequences.

# DICE

You've rolled

NUMBER

THIRTEEN:

don't

pursue it.

CRYSTAL BALL

A hazy shape
in the
CRYSTAL BALL
indicates
you're too unsure
of yourself
to proceed.

# TAROT

You've drawn
THE TEN
OF CUPS:
is this what
you really
want?

# ASTROLOGY

# jUPiTER

## gives you
## the okay.

CRYSTAL BALL

# THE
# CRYSTAL
# BALL

depicts an
empty purse:
don't
be greedy.

# PALMISTRY

According to
THE PALM
READER,
the girdle of Venus
indicates you should
rely on your
imagination—
your dream
can be a reality.

# TEA LEAVES

At the bottom of
YOUR
TEACUP
is a bird shape:
look outside
your
inner circle.

# PLAYING CARD

The card
you've chosen is
THE
JACK OF
CLUBS:
yes, but only
with assistance
from a loved one.

# TEA LEAVES

# THE TEA
# LEAVES
have formed

a clover:

indisputably

yes.

CRYSTAL BALL

# THE
# CRYSTAL
# BALL

indicates that fortune
will favor you,
if you leave
the past behind.

TAROT

You've drawn

# THE ACE
# OF CUPS:

let someone else

take the

initiative.

# PLAYING CARD

You've drawn
THE EİGHT OF
HEARTS:
you will succeed
if you use
discretion.

PSYCHİC

If today is Friday,

# THE PSYCHİC

says the

answer is yes.

TAROT

You've chosen

THE TOWER

CARD:

too much pride

may prevent it

from happening.

# PLAYING CARD

You've selected
THE ΤΕΠ ΟF
CLUBS:
it will prompt
someone from
the past to
reappear.

# TEA LEAVES

# THE
# TEA LEAVES

appear to form

a demon:

what you want

is not what

you need.

TAROT

You've drawn

THE QUEEN OF
SWORDS:

you may have

to go it alone.

PLAYING CARD

You've selected
THE ACE OF
SPADES:
try to live
without it.

# PSYCHIC

Listen to
THE PSYCHIC:
avoid it like
the plague.

# PALMISTRY

# THE PALM READER

observes a square palm and fingers: pay attention to the details.

# PLAYING CARD

You've drawn
THE QUEEN OF
SPADES:
look to a
dark-haired
woman
for the answer.

# CRYSTAL BALL

# THE
# CRYSTAL
# BALL

reveals a

magnifying glass:

step away and

examine your

alternatives.

# TEA LEAVES

# THE
# TEA LEAVES
have formed
the shape of
a pound sign:
only if you
can afford it.

DİCE

You've rolled

A TWELVE:

it will nourish

your soul.

# ASTROLOGY

THE SUN,
as center of
the universe,
guarantees
you'll be
admired for
your actions.

PLAYING CARD

You've drawn
THE TEN OF
SPADES:
it's not
up to you.

TAROT

You've drawn
THE KİΠG ΘF
SWΘRDS:
someone else
will have
the last word.

PSYCHIC

# THE
# PSYCHIC
# SAYS,
don't overlook
the details.

# PALMISTRY

# THE PALM READER

sees a starred palm:

you will be

successful

by virtue

of sheer talent.

TAROT

You've drawn

THE PRIΠCE
OF SWORDS:

watch for

unexpected turns

in the road.

# TEA LEAVES

# THE
## TEA LEAVES
have formed
the shape of a kite:
set your sights
even higher.

DICE

A roll of

TWELVE

means an

indisputable

yes.

# ASTROLOGY

# MERCURY

avows your wish

will be

granted

after

a reversal.

# ASTROLOGY

PISCES,
THE SIGN OF
THE FISH,

assures that

everything

will fall

into place.

# PALMISTRY

THE PALM
READER

has assessed

Chiron's bundle:

do it for

the good

of humanity.

TAROT

You've drawn
THE DEVİL
CARD:
someone is
trying to prevent
it from being so.

PLAYING CARD

You've selected
THE EİGH†
⊙F CLUBS:
you can't be
that naïve.

# DICE

You've rolled

AN ELEVEN:

give it a rest.

# ASTROLOGY

AQUARIUS,
the sign of the
Water Bearer,
recommends you
consider another
course of action.

# TAROT

You've drawn
THE
TEMPERANCE
CARD:
yes, but
with
moderation.

# TAROT

You've drawn
THE
DEATH
CARD:
what appears
to be out of reach
is anything but.

# PALMISTRY

THE PALM
READER
has interpreted
Diana's arrow:
get some rest first.

# DİCE

You've rolled

DOUBLE

FİVES:

await a

positive response

from a most

important

person.

# ASTROLOGY

CAPRICORN,
the sign of
the Goat,
advises you to
challenge
your limits.

# CRYSTAL BALL

The image in
THE CRYSTAL
BALL
is unmistakable:
you'll have
to improvise.

PLAYING CARD

You've selected
THE SEVEN
OF CLUBS:
it will help
improve
your karma.

# TAROT

You've chosen

# THE HANGED
# MAN CARD:

yes, through

sacrifice.

# TEA LEAVES

The tea leaves

form the

SHAPE ⊙F

A FİSH:

cast your

net wider.

PLAYING CARD

You've drawn
THE SIX OF
CLUBS:
it's not that
important.

TAROT

You've drawn
THE
STRENGTH
CARD:
you have the
power to
sort it out.

# PALMISTRY

# THE PALM READER

has analyzed
Neptune's
rocking horse:
a change in
perspective
is in order.

# PLAYING CARD

You've selected
THE FİVE ⊙F
CLUBS:
try it at
least once.

# CRYSTAL BALL

# IT'S CRYSTAL CLEAR:

you can

count on it.

# TEA LEAVES

At the bottom
OF YOUR
TEACUP
is an image
of a bat:
meditate about it
tonight.

# ASTROLOGY

SAGITTARIUS,
the sign of
the Centaur,
prompts you to forge
ahead no matter
what the cost.

# PSYCHIC

Only if you want
it bad enough, says
THE PSYCHIC.

# ASTROLOGY

SCORPIO,
the sign of
the Scorpion,
indicates
there's nothing
to worry about.

# TEA LEAVES

Relax . . .

only then will

THE TEA

LEAVES

yield an answer.

TAROT

# THE
# WHEEL-⊙F-
# FOR†UNE
# CARD

assures you it

will come to pass.

# PLAYING CARD

The card
you've drawn is
THE FOUR OF
CLUBS:
a change
is in the making.

# PALMISTRY

# THE PALM READER

observes a
mystic cross
in the palm:
have faith.

TAROT

# THE
# HERMIT
# CARD

urges you
to look
inward first.

DICE

You've rolled
AΠ EİGHT,
which indicates
that someone
is pressuring you.
Push them back.

# PLAYING CARD

# THE QUEEN OF HEARTS

urges you to follow
your heart instead
of what others say.

# PALMISTRY

# THE PALM READER

sees a butterfly shape

in the hand:

rely on the

help of

a stranger.

# PSYCHIC

# THE PSYCHIC

indicates yes,
but be on guard
against the
selfishness
of others.

# TAROT

You've drawn
THE ACE OF
WANDS.
Do you have
to be in charge?
If not,
step aside.

# PLAYING CARD

Your card is the
SIX OF
DIAMONDS:
have a
good cry first.

# TEA LEAVES

THE TEA
LEAVES
have formed
a mushroom shape;
try to look at it
through the eyes
of a child.

# PALMISTRY

According to
THE PALM
READER,
the Saturn (middle)
finger
indicates a
guilty conscience—
apologize first.

# PSYCHIC

# THE
# PSYCHIC'S
answer is
plain and simple:
no.

# TAROT

You've drawn
THE KING
OF CUPS:
the answer will
come to you
naturally.

# PALMISTRY

According to
THE PALM
READER,
the Jupiter (index)
finger indicates
you need to
tone it down.

# DICE

# THE DİCE
have rolled
off the table:
let it go.

# ASTROLOGY

# A LUNAR ECLIPSE

indicates uncertainty—
reconsider your
question
and ask again.

# CRYSTAL BALL

# THE
# CRYSTAL
# BALL

predicts you'll
get a lucky
break.

PLAYING CARD

# THE FIVE OF
# DIAMONDS

indicates an

unequivocal yes.

# PALMISTRY

According to
THE PALM
READER,
the life line
shows incredible
fortitude:
be patient.

PSYCHIC

# THE PSYCHIC

advises you to

make an offer

and see

what happens.

TAROT

You've drawn
THE QUEEN
OF CUPS:
your present goal
is unreachable.

PSYCHIC

# THE PSYCHIC
senses you are

not yet ready

for the answer.

# TEA LEAVES

A windmill
has appeared
among the
TEA LEAVES:
the situation will
change drastically
before it's resolved.

PSYCHIC

# THE PSYCHIC

has spoken:

not this year.

# ASTROLOGY

# THE STARS

urge you not

to delay.

DİCE

# A ROLL
# OF SIXTEEN

reveals the answer is yes,

but only if you

get to it

immediately.

# CRYSTAL BALL

According to
THE CRYSTAL
BALL,
a negative force
is keeping you
from success.

# PALMISTRY

# THE PALM
# READER

sees a crescent

in the hand:

act as if it's

already

happened.

# TAROT

You've drawn
THE PRİNCE
⊙F CUPS:
yes, with the help
of a man
who's not afraid
of his
feminine side.

# PLAYING CARD

You've selected the
THREE OF
DIAMONDS:
nothing ventured,
nothing gained.

PSYCHIC

# THE PSYCHIC

says to expect

your answer

to emerge

during a crisis.

# CRYSTAL BALL

According to
THE CRYSTAL
BALL,
someone else
has already made
the decision
for you.

# TEA LEAVES

A flower
has appeared
among the
TEA LEAVES:
take a fresh
approach.

# ASTROLOGY

MARS,
the planet of war,
urges you
to go after
what you desire.

TAROT

You've drawn
THE ACE OF
PENTACLES:
you will be rewarded
for your efforts.

PSYCHIC

# THE PSYCHIC

says, sooner

than you know.

# PLAYING CARD

You've drawn the
THREE OF
SPADES:
the answer to your
question
is a resounding yes.

# PALMISTRY

# THE PALM READER

sees a curving
marriage line:
the circumstances
will change
for the better.

# TEA LEAVES

# THE TEA
# LEAVES

have formed the

shape of a snake :

things are not

as they appear.

# CRYSTAL BALL

# THE
# CRYSTAL
# BALL

shows a
closed door:
is something
holding
you back?

# DICE

You've rolled
THE NUMBER
FOURTEEN:
a friend's help
will get you
through.

# ASTROLOGY

JUPITER,
the planet of
abundance,
blesses you with
a yes answer.

CRYSTAL BALL

# THE
# CRYSTAL
# BALL'S

answer:

more than you

can imagine.

# ASTROLOGY

# THE PLANET
# SATURN
indicates there's
turbulence
ahead if you do.

# DİCE

You've rolled
DOUBLE SIXES:
fortune is
favoring you,
so seize
the moment.

TAROT

You've drawn
THE KING OF
WANDS:
only if you
can maintain
control.

PSYCHIC

THE PSYCHIC

senses it's
already in
the works.

# PLAYING CARD

# THE ACE OF
# DIAMONDS
forecasts success
if you act
immediately.

# TEA LEAVES

# THE
# TEA LEAVES

have formed
an anchor shape:
assess your
financial situation
first.

# PALMISTRY

THE PALM
READER
sees dual
affection lines:
you can't
have it
both ways.

# CRYSTAL BALL

# THE
# CRYSTAL
# BALL

assures you will

gain that which

you seek.

# PALMISTRY

# THE PALM READER

has assessed
Diana's bow:
listen to your
hunches.

# DICE

You've rolled
ΠUMBER ΤΕΠ:
you will obtain
what you
wish for.

# ASTROLOGY

URANUS,
the planet of
revolution,
says yes, but it will
change your
life forever.

# CRYSTAL BALL

According to

# THE

# CRYSTAL

# BALL,

you may

rely on it.

# TAROT

You've drawn
THE QUEEN
OF WANDS:
don't bite the
hand that
feeds you.

# PSYCHIC

# THE
# PSYCHIC
# SENSES

you're about to
encounter a
fork in the road:
stick to the
well-trodden path.

# CRYSTAL BALL

# THE CRYSTAL
# BALL

shows a sand castle:
don't forget to
enjoy yourself.

# DICE

You've rolled
ΠUMBER FİVE:
learn from the
lessons of
the past.

PLAYING CARD

You've drawn
THE SİX OF
SPADES:
not with
that attitude.

# TAROT

You've drawn
THE PRINCESS
OF SWORDS:
keen judgment
is required.

# ABOUT THE AUTHOR

GEORGIA ROUTSIS SAVAS has been divining in some shape or form for as long as she can remember. ∞ Her broad-ranging career has taken her from composing advertising copy for *Ms.* magazine to writing fashion reports for CNN's hit show *Style With Elsa Klensch*. ∞ She writes a popular monthly horoscope column for *In Style* magazine, and in the past has written astro forecasts for an array of national magazines, including *Child*, *The New York Daily News Sunday Magazine* and *Sassy*. ∞ She is the author of one book, *Seventeen* magazine's *Total Astrology: What the Stars Say about Life and Love*. ∞ She also does private consultations, chart mapping and cosmic divination. ∞ These days, she gazes at the stars from her home on the North Carolina coast.